The Chinese New Year

by Cheng Hou-tien

Scissor cuts by the author

Holt, Rinehart and Winston • New York

Holt, Rinehart and Winston • New York
Copyright © 1976 by Cheng Hou-tien
All rights reserved, including the right to reproduce
this book or portions thereof in any form.
Published simultaneously in Canada by Holt, Rinehart
and Winston of Canada, Limited.
Printed in the United States of America

10   9   8   7   6   5   4   3

Library of Congress Cataloging in Publication Data
Cheng, Hou-tien.
    The Chinese New Year.
    SUMMARY: Briefly describes the most important
Chinese holiday, which signals the end of winter and the
coming of spring.
    1. New Year—China—Juvenile literature. (1. New
Year—China. 2. China—Social life and customs)
I. Title.
GT.4905.C45   394.2'683
ISBN 0-03-017511-9
    76-8229   10 9 8 7 6 5 4 3

pbk.   ISBN 0-03-048961-X
       79-10128   10 9 8 7 6 5 4 3 2 1

To my grandmother in Banfu

Introduction

The Chinese calendar is full of holidays. A single month can provide two or three occasions for celebration. Some holidays are more important than others. But the Chinese New Year, which has been celebrated for five thousand years, is by far the most festive and the most important. It signals the end of winter and the coming of spring.

The holiday goes on for days and days. There is the Little New Year, a time of preparation, the big five days of the New Year, a time of celebration, and the final three days of celebration— the Festival of Lanterns. People begin preparing for the five-day New Year celebration a month in advance. When the five days are over, preparations begin anew—for the Festival of Lanterns, which takes place about ten days later, when the moon is full. The first full moon of the year signals the arrival of spring. Thus, the whole New Year holiday lasts about a month and a half.

But the big five days are the main event. The daily flow of life comes to a halt as everyone celebrates the beginning of a new year.

The Little New Year

The last month of the year is spent preparing for the New Year festivities. It is a time of hard work and thanksgiving. Everything is made ready in advance—for shops and markets will be closed during the big five days and there will be no cooking beyond reheating. Chicken, fish and pork are salted and hung up to dry. Vegetables are pickled and duck eggs are preserved. Food is prepared for the streams of visitors who will be coming and going all the time.

A picture of Tsao-Chun, the god of the kitchen, hangs on the wall. He watches over everything. The family therefore tries hard to please him. Every corner of the house is scrubbed. A week before the New Year begins, Tsao-Chun's picture is taken down and burned. With a burst of firecrackers, the kitchen god is sent on his way to heaven, where he will report on the people of the house. The family has presented him with sweet cakes, fruits and treats, in the hope that he will be thinking sweet thoughts as he makes his report. A holiday spirit is everywhere—that is why this time is called the Little New Year.

When Tsao-Chun returns on New Year's Eve, the real celebration begins.

The Day of New Year's Eve

Families visit their friends and relatives to bid farewell to the old year.

New Year's Eve

There are two periods on New Year's Eve: the *hai,* from 9 P.M. until 11 P.M., and the *tsu,* from 11 P.M. to 1 A.M. During the *hai* period, incense is lit and placed on a table which has been arranged to meet the spirits who will descend to earth.

During the *tsu* period, offerings are made to the gods. A new picture of the kitchen god, Tsao-Chun, is hung up to welcome him, politely inviting him back to his shrine. The gods are asked to bring peace, health and prosperity.

The feast then takes place. Wine and refreshments are laid out. Inside, the lamps and candles give forth a calm light, while in the streets, the noise of the New Year's festivities and the bursts of firecrackers continue all night.

The Five Days
of the Chinese New Year

New Year's Day is primarily a family affair. Everyone puts on new clothes and wishes each other *Bai-nien*—Happy New Year.

Bī-nién

Gifts are exchanged. Packages of money, wrapped in red and gold, are given to children to spend as they wish during the holiday.

The stove is left on, heating food for the visitors who will arrive throughout the holiday. On this day, everyone eats *po-po*—boiled dumplings made from white flour. It is said that whoever bites into a dumpling and finds a surprise inside will have good fortune throughout the year.

On the second day of the New Year, family visits are returned. In each home large pine and cypress branches are placed in a vase and decorated with old coins, paper flowers, fruit charms and other adornments. This is the traditional "Money Tree"—a symbol of prosperity.

On the third day, the air crackles with firecrackers and the streets are packed with people watching the Dragon Dance. In this dance, a paper dragon is carried by people who "walk" the dragon around. One person runs ahead of the dragon, holding a white ball, sometimes called the pearl of fire.

This day also marks the beginning of the Lion Dance, which will go on through the fifth day. Men sharing a lion costume dance through the streets, accompanied by dancers and musicians. A young boy runs ahead of the lion teasing him, while people in the crowd throw firecrackers at the lion's feet.

The fourth day is much like the third day. On this day of open house, casual acquaintances, even strangers, may drop in for a visit.

The fifth day of the New Year ends the New Year's celebration. It is a day for visiting people who live far away, a day of travel and reunion. Life at home returns to normal. Food may be cooked again and shops are once more open.

The Lantern Festival or Feast of the First Full Moon

The Festival of Lanterns begins about ten days later, with the first full moon of the new year. It lasts three days—one day before, the day of and the day after the new moon. Lanterns are suspended from storefronts and homes, and doorways are decorated with glass beads and colored lamps. Honoring the full moon, women wear white, and put on their pearls. Little round white pastries called moon cakes are eaten.

The Chinese Zodiac

The first day of the Chinese new year falls on the first day of the new moon after the sun enters Aquarius. On the Christian Gregorian calendar, which we use in the Western world, it would fall somewhere between January 21 and February 20.

Unlike the Western zodiac, which is divided into twelve months, the Chinese zodiac is a twelve-year cycle. Each year is named after an animal. The animal which represents the year of a person's birth becomes his animal sign.

The Chinese have for centuries believed that a person's animal sign determines much of his character and destiny. Decisions about such important issues as marriage, friendship and business are almost always made according to the guidelines of one's animal sign.

Year	Zodiac Animal	
1979	Sheep	
1980	Monkey	
1981	Cock	
1982	Dog	
1983	Pig	
1984	Rat	
1985	Ox	
1986	Tiger	
1987	Rabbit	
1988	Dragon	
1989	Snake	
1990	Horse